Fiction Attic Press

Novel Starter

50 Days of Exercises and Advice to Get Your Novel off the Ground

FICTION ATTIC

First published by Fiction Attic Press in 2017

ISBN: 978-1-945753-08-4

This book was professionally typeset on Reedsy.
Find out more at reedsy.com

Contents

II   Halfway There Self-Assessment

III Days 27-50

IV   Next Steps

Introduction

Sometimes the hardest part about being a writer is putting the first words on the page. *Novel Starter: 50 Days of Inspiration to Get Your Novel off the Ground*, will spark your imagination and help you turn your ideas into stories and chapters. Each day, instead of opening your notebook to a blank page, you will open it to a possibility.

The book is also designed as a crash course in narrative craft. Throughout the book, you'll find a series of **Craft Keys** that will demystify the fundamental elements of narrative craft: dialogue, characterization, point of view, description, voice, setting, and more. Even if you've taken creative writing courses in the past, the craft keys provide useful ways to think about the building blocks of fiction.

Every day, you'll find a new exercise to help you face the page. Use this book every day for fifty days. Each day, try to write for at least twenty minutes. Half an hour is even better, and 45 minutes is better still, but I want you to make this promise to yourself, right now:

For the next 50 days, I will write for 20 minutes each day.

Go ahead, say it out loud. You'll be amazed how much you can accomplish in 20 focused minutes. Suddenly a sentence will turn into a paragraph, a paragraph into a page. Fifty days from now, you will open this workbook to find something wonderful: pages and pages of your own words--written, I hope, with an eye for detail but also with a sense of creative abandon. It may not look like a novel quite yet; but it will look like a solid body of original work. You will have seeded the the ground from which your novel will grow.

And somewhere in this workbook, after you are finished, there's a very good chance you'll find a great short story that just needs a bit of revision before it's ready to be sent into the world.

Where are you going?

Don't think too much, at first, about where the story is going. The exercises in the first half of the workbook are designed to be open-ended. Instead of beginning each exercise with the thought, "Now I'm going to write my novel," begin with the idea, "I'm going to see where this takes me." This is especially true with Free Flow Exercises (more on that later).

While this workbook is focused on novel writing, every one of these exercises may be adapted for nonfiction. If the prompt is "write about a time when your character was angry," you may choose instead to write from memory, delving into your own life stories. If you find the same character, real or imagined, popping up in various exercises, go with it; you may have found the protagonist of your novel.

You may skip around among the prompts, or you may follow the structure outlined in the workbook, consecutively from Day 1 to Day 2 to Day 3, all the way to Day 50. The first few exercises are intentionally sense or emotion driven, designed to help you get your pen moving quickly and ignite the creative impulse. I recommend beginning with these before moving on to the more complex exercises.

Some exercises focus on specific aspects of narrative craft, such as dialogue, point of view, and dramatic tension; if you're in the mood to work on your characterization skills, for example, you can choose one of the exercises specifically marked *characterization.* Please note that some prompts are meant to follow upon the previous day's exercise; follow-up exercises are always marked as such.

Halfway through: take your pulse

On Day 26, you will find the **Halfway There Self-Assessment**. If you're doing the prompts in order, you'll naturally come upon this page halfway through your 50 days of writing practice. If you're skipping around in the book, please head directly to Day 26 after you have completed 25 days of prompts. Please take time to follow the instructions for the Halfway There Self-Assessment. Don't worry if it takes you a few days to complete. The Self-Assessment is designed to help you identify your strengths, celebrate your best work, and face your writing fears.

Three Kinds of Exercises

Free Flow

Free flow exercises are about moving the pen. They are about writing until your hand hurts. They are about finding the magic of inspiration. They are about feeling the words, not making sense of them. Free flow exercises, like all of the exercises in this book, can be done more than once. Each time, they will render wildly different results. If you are like most writers I know, you have days that seem too overwhelming to get a single word down on paper, days when you feel uninspired, days when your inner critic says, "I'll never be a writer." I recommend the free flow exercises for these days. I've used them for years in my creative writing classes, and as the pens scratch across the pages, I can't help feeling that the Muse has landed. Free flow exercises help you get back to the joy of writing.

Ten Minute

Ten-minute exercises appear periodically throughout the workbook. "But," you protest, "you made me promise to write for 20 minutes a day!" Yes, I did, and I'm not letting you off the hook. But sometimes, no matter how committed you are to writing, you simply cannot find more than ten minutes. Even as a full-time writer, I have those days. I recommend saving the 10-minute exercises for days when you're so overwhelmed that you're tempted not to write anything at all. There is a great value in honoring the promise you made to yourself write every day, even if you don't write for as long as you would like.

Chapter/Scene

Chapter/Scene exercises appear in the latter half of the workbook. You'll find exercises that ask you to write fully fleshed out scenes and chapters. Don't panic. You're not expected to churn out 12 pages in a day. When a prompt says, "Write a chapter about," think in terms of a very short scene or chapter—aim for 1,000 to 1,200 words. Writing a fully-fleshed-out chapter allows you to complete a narrative arc in a short period of time. It also allows you to enjoy the process without too much pressure, which is what this workbook is all about.

Several of these exercises are based on stories in the anthology *Flash Fiction: 72 Very Tiny Stories* (edited by James Thomas, Denise Thomas, and Tom Hazuka, and published by Norton in 1992). I have taught from this anthology many times and have always found my writing students in both undergraduate and graduate level courses to be particularly responsive to these tiny narrative gems. It is by no means necessary to read the stories that inspired the exercises before you complete them, but you're welcome to do so for examples of some very short stories that push all the right buttons. I would recommend purchasing the book, but reading a particular story only after you have completed the corresponding exercise. Since publishing this workbook, I have edited two flash fiction anthologies: Flash in the Attic: 33 Very Short Stories, and Flash in the Attic 2: 44 Very Short Stories. I recommend both for students of flash fiction.

While doing the chapter/scene exercises, you may well find yourself writing beyond the1200 words I recommend here. That's fine! In fact, I encourage it. The goal of these exercises is to inspire you to write a complete chapter, be it three pages or 30.

I

Days 1-25

1

Craft Key 1: Description

Remember to favor the concrete over the abstract. *Red balloon* is more memorable than *balloon*. *Chocolate cake* is more likely to stir the senses than *dessert*.

That said, remember that you don't have to use every adjective you can think of. Choose your details wisely. *Red balloon* is not only better than *balloon*; it is also better than *red helium striped balloon*. And, in writing (if not in life), a simple *chocolate cake* is often better than a *three-layer German chocolate cake with vanilla piping and raspberry filling* ,unless your character happens to be a pastry chef, in which case you can pile on the culinary details with abandon. Context is everything. If you find yourself writing about a rose-colored paisley sofa, ask yourself if those rose-colored paisleys add anything beyond window-dressing to the story.

Now, before you begin the exercises, use this simple list of words to generate a few concrete details. Simply write a sentence or two for each word in which the general becomes specific.

- a girl
- a bus
- a house
- a table

- the weather

2

Day 1

Setting & Description

Write about the kitchens of your childhood. Who populated them?
What are your sharpest memories of those moments? It's okay if these
scenes veer from reality. One of the great joys of writing is allowing
the real places and events of our lives to take an imaginary turn, in
which we control the story.

3

Day 2

Setting & Description

Write about something that took place in the middle of the night. Allow the reader to experience night without ever using the word "night."

4

Day 3

Setting & Conflict

Now write about something that took place in the heat and brightness of midday. Begin by describing the setting, and then place a character in the setting. How do the oppressive heat and light influence the character's actions?

For an excellent example, see chapter 6 of *The Stranger*, by Albert Camus.

5

Day 4

Characterization

Write about a time when your protagonist was very angry. What motivated the anger? How did the character display or conceal his or her anger?

6

Day 5

Write a scene that takes place one week after the scene you wrote for Day 4. What subtle (or not so subtle) changes have taken place in the character in the intervening days? Has his/her situation changed? Has the anger subsided, or has it festered? How have the character's relationships been altered by the episode?

7

Craft Key 2: Characterization

Character is revealed in three primary ways:
- appearance
- dialogue
- action

I've listed them here in ascending order.

Appearance

While writing what your character looks like may be the easiest task, it is really the least important. Give your readers a glimpse of your character and move on. Don't get too bogged down in hair, eyes, clothing, etc. What is left unsaid will be filled in by the reader's imagination.

Dialogue

Dialogue allows us to understand what a character is thinking, and often provides dramatic tension when what the character says is different from what he or she thinks or feels.

Actions

Actions speak louder than words. In fiction, as if life, actions provide clues for how to understand an individual. Actions reveal what a character is made of. Actions that are in conflict with a character's words (dialogue) or self-image (as revealed through thoughts) also serve as an important source of dramatic tension

Someone who drives alone down a country road at night when angry is a very different from someone who punches the object of his anger in the face or slams a plate against the wall. Someone who says, "Family is the most important thing to me" but cheats on his wife or skips his kids' sporting events reveals an internal conflict, or at the very least a talent for self-deception.

8

Day 6

Characterization

Many people have a box of keepsakes–letters, photographs, awards, etc. Explore this box for your protagonist.

- What does the box look like, and where is it kept?
- Write about each item it contains.
- How did your character acquire each item?
- Why did she keep each item?
- What did each item mean to her at the time?
- What do these items mean to her now?

If you have trouble doing this for your character, begin it as a memoir exercise, using your own personal keepsake box. This may help you get into the flow of writing about your character's keepsakes.

9

Day 7

Characterization & Conflict

Now, imagine that the keepsake box has been lost, stolen, or burned in a fire.
- Which item hurts the most to lose, and why?
- Does the character try to replace it? Why or why not?
- Whom does he/she tell about the loss? How does that person react?
- From whom does he/she hide the loss? Why?

10

Day 8

Point of View & Description

Write about something your protagonist saw and has been unable to forget. Use the first person present, as if the scene is unfolding before your protagonist's at this moment. Use all five senses.

11

Day 9

Characterization & Belief

Make a list of five things you believe deeply to be true. These things can be fact-based (the planet is getting warmer) or value-driven (people are basically good).

1.
2.
3.
4.
5.

Choose one item from your list. Now, write a scene in which a character tries to convince another person, or a group of people, that this thing is false. (For example, if you wrote "People are basically good," have your character try to convince someone that people are basically bad.)

12

Day 9 (cont.)

Choose one item from your list. Now, write a scene in which a character tries to convince another person, or a group of people, that this thing is false. (For example, if you wrote "People are basically good," have your character try to convince someone that people are basically bad.)

13

Day 10

Characterization, Description, and Conflict

Describe your protagonist's first meeting with someone who would later become a close friend. Then describe your protagonist's first meeting with someone who would later become an adversary.

14

Day 11

Dialogue

Write a conversation between two people who are in conflict about something specific. Do not explicitly state what they are in conflict about, but make it so that a careful reader will gradually come to understand. Keep the exchanges short: do not let either character say more than 15 words at a time.

You can play with this. For example, let each character say only 10 words at a time, five words at a time, etc.

For an example of a maddeningly oblique yet terrifically layered conversation between two characters, read Hemingway's classic short story, "Hills Like White Elephants."

15

Day 12

Point of View

Write about a significant event in your protagonist's childhood or adolescence from the point of view of the protagonist's mother/father/guardian/friend.

Allow yourself to fully inhabit your point-of-view character's feelings. Attempt to see the moment entirely through the point-of-view character's eyes.

16

Craft Key 3: Dramatic Tension

Dramatic tension is the lifeblood of narrative, and it is essential to establish it in the opening pages of a novel. The reader knows that *something* is going to happen, but we don't know what, and that is what keeps us reading.

There must be a sense of trouble or impending trouble from the very beginning. Take the opening line of The Trial, by Franz Kafka:

> *Someone must have slandered Josef K., for one morning, without having done anything truly wrong, he was arrested.*

Or the first three, brief lines of The Stranger, by Albert Camus:

> *Maman died today. Or yesterday maybe. I don't remember.*

Not only do we have in these three lines a death of someone presumably close to the narrator, but we also have a problem of memory: the speaker does not remember exactly when his mother died. Why and how did she die? Why does he not remember? Such promising conflict, so many questions raised, all in a very few words.

An excellent example of prolonged dramatic tension building up to a tragic event can be found in Ayelet Waldman's novel Red Hook Road.

17

Day 13

Dramatic Tension

A character arrives home to find something unexpected—a situation, person, or thing.

First, write a few sentences building up to the moment when the character sees/hears the unexpected thing.

18

Day 13 (cont.)

Next, write the moment when she makes the discovery. Describe it through your character's eyes.

19

Day 13 (cont.)

Finally, write her internal reaction to this discovery. How does it affect her? Change her? Going further, how does it change the direction of the story?

20

Day 14

Pacing: Scene vs. Summary

Tell the story of the most important moment in your character's life in two pages or more. Use sensory details and, if applicable, use dialogue. Take it slowly. Make the **scene** as concrete as possible. The goal is to allow the reader to experience this moment with your character.

21

Day 15

Reflection

Surely you've heard the old adage, "Show, don't tell." While the advice has merit, I've seen writers choke up when it came to writing about a character's thoughts or feelings because they were so worried that they might be telling.

There is, at it turns out, a time to tell, a time for reflection. I want you to do that now.

Read back over what you wrote for Day 14, the scene of the most important moment in your character's life. Now write about what all of that meant to you or to your character. How did it change him or her?

Think about the lens of time. Is your character's perspective on that moment now very different from what it was at the time it happened? In retrospect, how did the moment change your character?

22

Day 16

Pacing: Scene vs. Summary

You have now fully explored one of the most important moments in your character's life. You have compressed time by slowing down to focus with intricate detail on a single point.

Now, tell the story of your character's life, in a page or two. This is an exercise in pacing. The writer is continually deciding what to gloss over, and what to expand upon. The best scenes take us inside a significant moment that is revealed completely, with a beginning, middle, and end. But not everything deserves a scene. The funeral of a loved one, for example, may constitute an entire chapter in a novel, while the protagonist's years in college may constitute only a couple of pages.

23

Craft Key 4: Point of View

There are two things to consider when choosing the point of view of your novel:
Who is telling the story?
From what distance?

There are four primary points of view you might choose for your novel:

1. First person
2. Limited third person
3. Omniscient
4. Second person (rarely used, as it can feel very claustrophobic!)

Whatever point of view you choose, one of the biggest mistakes you can make is to suddenly shift point of view within a scene or chapter, thereby interrupting the fictional dream. This is particularly true with first person narration. If your novel is told from the point of view of a particular character, you must be careful not to break character by suddenly revealing something that your point of view character wouldn't logically know. The moment you slip into someone else's mind, or see through someone else's eyes, the gig is up, and the reader is left wondering, "What just happened?"

To be in command of your story, you must be inc command of point of view.

24

Day 17

Point of View

Write about a terrible deed from the point of view of someone who doesn't find the deed objectionable. Why: literature, like life, is populated with characters who don't see themselves as others see them. Just think of Humbert Humbert, the infamous and infinitely silver-tongued hero/villain of Nabokov's *Lolita*.

25

Day 18

Dialogue

Write a scene of rejection entirely in dialogue.

   Craft note: dialogue consists of the words that are said, in addition to the dialogue tags (he said/she said), and the gestures the characters use while speaking.

   "Get down from there right now," she said, waving her arms frantically
   is dialogue.

   I was sitting in the tree when my mother appeared, sweating and belliger-ent in her good Sunday shoes
   is narrative (i.e., anything that isn't dialogue).

26

Day 19

Dialogue, Conflict, & Setting

Two friends are in love with the same person. One of them (Friend A) describes his/her feelings to the other (Friend B). Friend A does not know about Friend B's feelings for the person. Friend B tries not to let on how s/he feels.

Write the conversation. Include details of setting (where does the conversation take place), as well as gestures.

27

Day 20

Secondary characters

Usually, we know who our protagonist is before we begin writing. The novel often begins with an idea of a particular person in a particular (conflict-filled) situation.

But a single character does not a novel make. Where do secondary and peripheral characters come from? Sometimes they are based on people we know, and sometimes they seem to arrive from thin air. I like the thin air characters the best. But how do we conjure them?

Think of the people who are most memorable to you. Often, we remember them in certain moments, certain situations, but we also tend to remember one or two identifying gestures, speech patterns, or habits: the guy at the office who always flips his tie over his shoulder before drinking his coffee, the lady on the subway who is always humming the same tune.

Today, you're going to try to conjure a character from thin air. To do so, fill in the blanks, and then keep writing.

Every time I saw her, she was wearing the same .... She used to say things like, "...."

28

Day 21

Character in Crisis

Write a scene in which a character is somehow immobilized. The character may be stuck in a stalled subway car, confined to a bed or wheelchair, locked in a room. The possibilities are endless.

   How does your character confront this minor or major crisis? How does he or she respond to the obstacle put in his or her way?

29

Craft Key 5: Plot & Pacing

Plot is, simply stated, the sequence of events.

Pacing refers to the speed and tempo of the narrative.

Pacing may be rapid, meandering, or slow.

While pacing shifts from scene to scene depending on the action of the scene, the overall pacing of the novel should feel consistent. Most successful thrillers, for example, are praised for being "fast-paced."

Patterning is a term I use to think about how a novel is laid out. It involves the frequency with which certain themes and subplots emerge, the order in which these pieces are presented.

30

Day 22

Freedom

Read what you wrote yesterday. Now, get the person out of confinement.
- How does your character get out?
- Does she do it alone, or with the help of another person?
- Is she truly free of the confinement, or does she only think she is free?

31

Day 23

Write about someone your protagonist misses very much. How does your character attempt to get in touch with this person? Or perhaps your character doesn't try to get in touch--why?

Some of the best dramatic tension comes from failed or fraught relationships. In this exercise, if nothing comes to you immediately, let your own experience be your guide!

32

Day 24

Fill in the blanks

Let's try another fill-in-the-blank exercise. The beauty of fill-in-the-blank is that it takes you somewhere totally unexpected. It's also a great way to find an unexpected aspect of your voice, and to open up narrative possibilities.

This one is inspired by Stuart Dybek's "Lights."

Begin your story by filling in the blanks, and then just keep writing. Eventually, you'll want to get rid of the borrowed words in order to make the story entirely your own.

In (season), waiting for (something/someone), we'd (...). Sometimes (...). But there were times when (....)

33

Day 25

10-minute free flow

On the last day of the first half of your journey into your novel, you're going to riff. Think of it as narrative jazz.

For this exercise, you'll need to time yourself--I like to use a smartphone app, but a kitchen timer will do. For each portion of the exercise, write for one minute. When the minute is up, turn the page and move on immediately to the next prompt, even if you're in the middle of a sentence. Don't worry about how or even if the separate pieces connect. Just write. Before you begin, close your eyes for a minute and try to get into the mind of your protagonist. Then tackle the exercise in the first person.

Write about falling.

34

Free flow, part 2

Write about the last person you fought with.

35

Free flow, part 4

Write about the last thing that terrified you.

36

Free flow, part 5

Write about a work of art.

37

Free flow, part 3

Write about the last thing you lost.

38

Free flow, part 7

Write about the last thing you found.

39

Free flow, part 6

Write about a place that is very hot.

40

Free flow, part 8

Write about a place that is very cold.

41

Free flow, part 9

Write about your father.

42

Free flow, part 10

Write about flying.

II

Halfway There Self-Assessment

43

Day 26: Halfway There Self-Assessment

Congratualations! You are now halfway through your fifty days of writing. You should be proud of what you've accomplished. This is a great day to read through what you've written. It will certainly take more than your allotted twenty minutes or so to read all of the completed exercises, so I encourage you to carve out time today, or perhaps tonight in bed before you turn out the light, to read through your work so far and answer the first question below. Because the self-assessment exercise includes several questions that require a good deal of thought and might produce lengthy answers, feel free to take a few days to do it. You might, for example, answer one question each day while continuing to do your daily writing exercises.

Which piece did I most enjoy writing? Why?

44

Self-Assessment, part 2

Which exercise was the most difficult to complete? Why? Are there certain craft elements that I find more daunting than others?

45

Self Assessment, part 3

Which piece is the closest to being a completed chapter? Are any of the completed exercises a good opening chapter for my novel?

46

Self Assessment, part 4

Which characters did I write about the most?

Why am I drawn to these real or imagined characters?

What makes this/these characters complex enough to carry the weight of my novel?

47

Self Assessment, part 5

What have I learned about my own writing, and my writing process, along the way?

48

Self-Assessment, part 6

Did I keep my promise to myself to write every day? If not, what held me back? What was the most difficult obstacle standing in the way of my writing every day? How can I confront this obstacle the next time I face it?

III

Days 27-50

49

Craft Key 6: Dialogue & Point of View

In addition to actions, the way characters speak and the things they say reveal multitudes about their personality, background, values, and motivations.

Dialogue gives shape to scenes and shows interactions between characters. Dialogue is particularly important when the narrator of the novel is not omniscient. Only an omniscient narrator knows what everyone is thinking and feeling and is at liberty to reveal these things to the reader at any time.

If your novel is written in the first person or limited third person, on the other hand, dialogue is a crucial way of revealing what other characters are thinking. The words that come out of the characters' mouths form a logical connection between the internal and the external. In a first person novel we can only be inside the mind of the narrator; dialogue is essential in providing a glimpse into other characters' thoughts.

50

Day 27

Write a scene in which a man (or boy) questions a woman (or girl) about her mother. Pay attention not only to the character's words, but also to their gestures. Even though the woman or girl is off the page, we should get to know her through the dialogue between the other two characters.

51

Day 28

Found

Imagine that your character comes upon a battered notebook that has been left on a deserted park bench, or in a motel room, or in the seat back on the airplane--anywhere.

Written (or typed, or scrawled) across the front of the notebook is the word, "Private." What does your character do?

You might want to begin this exercise by writing about the place where the notebook is found, and what the character is doing there.

For the moment, don't describe the contents of the notebook itself. We are focused here on setting up the scene and learning about how our character responds to this unusual situation.

52

Day 29

Yesterday, you had a character discover a notebook marked *private*. You described the setting in which the notebook was found, and you described the character's reaction. Now, write the contents of the notebook itself. There's no limit to what your found notebook can contain: it might be a diary, letters, plans for a bicycle/bomb/rocket/time machine.

The "found text" has a long literary tradition. I recommend *Death of a Beekeeper*, by Lars Gustafsson, and *Gould's Book of Fish*, by Richard Flannagan. In *No One You Know*, I used a found text (the mathematical notebook of the narrator's sister) as a key to unlocking a mystery of the narrator's sister's death. Found texts are a great deal of fun to play with.

53

Day 30

This exercise is inspired by Vicki Lindner's "Proud Flesh." It's another fun way to find a new chapter in your novel that both reveals character and propels the plot along.

Begin with the skeleton of this sentence, fill in the blanks, and keep writing.

When (name) moved from ... to ... , he/she thought he/she ought to learn how to ....

54

Day 31

Write a scene in which a single important moment in your protagonist's life is set against the backdrop of some larger (national or international) event.

An excellent example of this is "Snow," by Julia Alvarez.

Charles Frasier's Cold Mountain is set against the backdrop of the end of the Civil War.

Jonathan Saffron Foer's Extremely Loud and Incredibly Close features a young protagonist whose father was killed in the World Trade Center attacks.

For Golden State, a novel about divorce, I chose the setting of modern-day California. The novel takes place the day the citizens of California vote on whether or not to secede from the United States.

Setting your novel against the backdrop of a larger historical or fictional event allows you to broaden the novel's scope. It also makes for interesting metaphorical possibilities.

55

Day 32

Habits & Rituals

Write about a bad habit your protagonist has, and why he or she is unable to break it.

An alternative: write about a ritual your protagonist practices daily, weekly, or yearly.

56

Craft Key 7: Tips for Effective Dialogue

- Avoid overly descriptive dialogue tags like "growled" and "hissed." A simple he said/she said is almost always preferable to a descriptive dialogue tag. Dialogue tags should be almost invisible, allowing us to hear the characters' voices (rather than the author's).
- Break up long sections of dialogue with gestures.
- When two people are speaking, allow for a quick back-and-forth if it fits the characters and the scene, rather than allowing one character to go on for too long without interruption.
- Don't have character's say one another's names when they're engaged in conversation, unless it's necessary to do so for emphasis. Doing so tends to sound stilted, as if the dialogue belongs in a soap opera.

57

Day 33

Not so ordinary

In Ray Bradbury's classic novel *Fahrenheit 451*, the duty of firemen is not to put out fires, but rather to start them. Specifically, they are charged with setting fire to books. Fahrenheit 451, you may remember, is the temperature at which a book's pages begin to burn.

Write a chapter in which an ordinary term (such as fireman) is turned on its head, taking on an entirely different meaning within the fictional world.

58

Day 34

Write down something your character would never do. Then write a story or chapter titled "How to _____."
Fill in the blank with that thing you would never do.

59

Day 35

Write a scene that involves a natural disaster.

This exercise is inspired by "What Happened During the Ice Storm," by Jim Heynen.

60

Day 36

Write a romantic scene set in a strange place, a place that seems anathema to love.

61

Day 37

Write a scene in which a single object poses a threat to a relationship.

This exercise is inspired by Jay Openheimer's story "The Paring Knife," in which a paring knife falls behind the refrigerator during a terrible fight between a man and a woman. The knife remains there for a long time, and when the husband finds it again, it serves as a symbol of the disruption in their marriage, and his desperate desire to forget it.

The exercise allows you to play with the power of a certain physical object as an "objective correlative" in your novel.

62

Day 38

Write down five words you love.

63

Day 38 (cont)

Write down five words you hate.

64

Day 38 (cont)

Now, write a scene that takes place in the rain. Include all of the words you love, and one of the words you hate.

65

Day 39

Make a list of five action verbs. Then turn the page.

66

Day 39 (cont)

Choose one of the action verbs from the previous page, and write a scene that begins with the line:

"Lately (character name) notices that she (action verb) more."

This exercise is inspired by "Vines" by Kenneth Bernard.

67

Day 40

Conflict

Write a scene in which your character is powerless to prevent some impending disaster about which s/he is fully aware.

This exercise is inspired by "Nadine at 35: A Synopsis," by Jo Sapp.

68

Day 41

Today, you'll be taking a break from scene writing to do a free flow exercise. This exercise may be a quick one, but it's spread over several pages so that you won't read ahead.

For this exercise, you'll need a timer. For each portion of the exercise, you'll write for two minutes. When the two minutes are over, move on immediately to the next prompt, even if you're in the middle of a sentence. Don't worry about how or even if the separate pieces connect. Just write. Begin here:

Describe one beautiful thing. Include a color in your description.

69

Day 41 (cont)

Write about the best food your character ever tasted.

70

Day 41 (cont)

Write about a promise your character once broke.

71

Day 41 (cont)

Write about your character's biggest fear.

72

Day 41 (cont)

Write about a moment of intense humiliation your character experienced.

73

Day 41 (cont.)

Okay, you've completed your ten minutes. But you don't have to stop there. If you've allotted more writing time today, read through the writing that you just did, pick a place where you stopped in the middle of a sentence or the middle of a thought, and keep writing.

74

Day 42

Write a scene or chapter filled with menace, with a sense of dread for something that is going to happen.

75

Day 43

Write a scene in which your protagonist finally gets/achieves something he or she has wanted for a very long time.

76

Day 44

In *The Death of a Beekeeper*, the beautifully humane and intellectually playful novella about disease, death, and the noble desire to "begin again," Lars Gustafsson uses lists to reveal the protagonist's most intimate self. There are lists about beekeeping, about expenses, about all sorts of details of his daily life.

Today, you'll be making lists. This exercise is comprised of three lists.

Begin by making a list of everything in your character's car. If you or the character doesn't have a car, choose a place where the character spends a lot of time: at his desk, in his bedroom, etc.

77

Day 44 (cont)

Now make a list of books your character holds dear, OR a list of favorite songs.

78

Day 44 (cont.)

Finally, make a list of things the character has thrown away in the last week.

79

Day 44 (cont.)

Now, choose one item from each of the three lists you've created for
Day 44, and write a scene using all three items.
   What do these items and the character's relationship to them reveal
about the character?

80

Day 45

Make a list of impossible occurrences, or occurrences that are at least impossible in the world as we know it. For example, you might take a scientific fact and state its opposite: the sun is cold, oxygen is poisonous to humans, dinosaurs are common household pets.

You might also include physically impossible situations; an example would be Gregor Samsa waking up as a cockroach in "The Metamorphosis."

81

Day 46

Choose one item on your list from Day 45.

Now, describe a world in which this impossibility is a reality. Rather than treating the premise as something extraordinary, however, treat it is commonplace.

In other words, don't write, "The residents of Cleveland were shocked to discover the dinosaurs in their back yards." Instead, write, "Don Smith, owner of Smith's Fine Asian Imports, went out every Saturday morning at dawn to feed rats to his dinosaur. He had been doing this for fifteen years..."

Even if you've never been interested in writing science fiction, this exercise is a great way to force yourself to think about how to **make the strange seem normal.** If you develop the skill of providing a realistic context and credibility to completely unrealistic/unbelievable situations, you will become adept at luring readers into your fictional dream.

82

Day 47

You may be familiar with *The Book of Laughter and Forgetting*, by Milan Kundera. From the opening paragraph of this politically charged novel, when faithful Comrade Clementis is hanged for treason and erased from the history books and photographs, one is plunged into a metaphorically dense story about truth and lies on both a personal and public scale, and humankind's tragic tendency toward forgetting.

Writing, at its heart, is an act of memory. We mine our own memories for details, characters, and emotional truths. With our words, we seek to create a fictional or real landscape that will be remembered by the reader.

Write a scene or chapter about memory. You may write about loss of memory, or about a character who is plagued by a particular memory, or about a memory that provides some kind of peace or offers a solution to a problem.

Day 48

Where I Come From

There's a great Tom Petty song called "Southern Accents," a song about identity, and about home, and about the things that remain even long after we have left our place of origin.

Where do you come from? Maybe you stayed, or maybe you left long ago. Either way, where you come from matters deeply to a writer.

One of the biggest things you can do for yourself is to find your Yoknapatawpha--the place that formed you, the place your writing will always, somehow, come home to. Faulkner's was Mississippi. Richard Yates's was suburban New York. Sherwood Anderson's was Winesburg, Ohio.

Today's exercise is really an exercise for every day, because the more you write, the more you will find this place cropping up in your stories. **Write about where you come from, or where your character comes from** (maybe they are one and the same). Make the place real by using all of the senses.

84

Day 49

Yesterday, you wrote about your Yoknapotawpha, the place where you and/or your character comes from.

Now, write about why you (or your character) stayed, or why you left, or why you will always (or never) return.

85

Day 50

The Search

We'll end with an exercise inspired by one of my favorite novels, *The Moviegoer* by Walker Percy. In this classic tale of love and longing in New Orleans, our gentleman narrator, Binx Bolling, woos his secretary, falls for his cousin, and muses lyrically on the nature of the search. "To become aware of the possibility of a search is to be onto something," he says. "Not to be onto something is to be in despair."

Writing is in itself a form of searching. You go off in search of the subject, the character, the story. The search you end with is rarely the one you began with. As the search evolves, so does the seeker. You may find that what you thought you wanted to write about isn't your true subject at all, or that the person you believed stood at the heart of the story is really a peripheral character, while someone else deserves to take center stage. Maybe your story about boats turns out to be a story about longing, but the theme doesn't occur to you until you were halfway in.

I hope you'll take a few days at least to complete your final exercise: **Write a scene or chapter about a search.**
But before you begin, look through the workbook for inspiration

from the characters and scenes you have created.

IV

Next Steps

86

I finished the workbook. Now what?

Congratulations on writing a short piece every day for 50 days! Remember, most novels take months or years to complete. **Every great novel begins somewhere, and yours might have begun within the pages of this book.**

Don't stop now. Keep going. ~~Try The Paperclip Method: The No-Outline Novel Workb~~ook, which will help you see the bigger picture, generate more material, create a compelling plot, and shape your scenes into a novel.

Go back and read each of the scenes you completed in the second half of the workbook. Which one makes you think, "Wow, did I really write that?" Take that piece and revise it. Make it sharper. Get rid of bulky language and clichés, but keep all the good stuff.

I think of Frederick Barthelme's excellent advice in *The 39 Steps: A Primer on Story Writing*: "Make up a story, screw around with it, paste junk on it, needle the characters, make them say queer stuff, go bad places, insert new people at inopportune moments."

Now, submit the piece as a flash fiction to a literary journal. It can't hurt. Yes, you're writing for the sheer joy of it, but if you're like most writers I know, you'd also like to be read. Even though you're working on a novel, a small publication can be a big boost to your confidence. For a list of literary magazines accepting short fiction, go to http://newpages.com or http://pw.org/literary_magazines.

87

Do-over

They say that in life there are no do-overs. Fortunately, in writing, do-overs are part of the process. We call that revision.

Choose one exercise that you feel you made a mess of, and do it all over again.

Throw away the original; there are more words where those came from. I once threw away a 400-page novel-in-progress because I finally came to the conclusion that nothing short of an act of God would save that book. And I figured God had more important things to attend to. As soon as I tossed it, I felt freed of the albatross. I started a new novel, which I completed in a year--the fastest by far I've ever written a book.

Try it now. Crumple the page, and put it in the actual trash can (don't just scoot it over to the little icon on your Macbook). You'll be amazed how good it will make you feel.

88

One Great Sentence

And a Pat on the Back

One by one, read through all 50 exercises and, in each one, underline at least one great sentence. Then underline at least one great image. So much of the work of being a writer involves knowing what to keep. By the time I finish a book, dozens of pages have fallen by the wayside. These are pages over which I labored, pages that, at one point, I may have even loved. But the beautiful thing about words is that they are in such abundant supply. You can afford to say goodbye to some of your sentences, because there will always be more. But there are some sentences you'd be a fool to lose. Some sentences so beautiful that just thinking of them makes you glow.

Most of us are pretty good at being our own worst critic. But the critics for the major newspapers don't just offer condemnation; they also offer praise. When you're being too hard on yourself, thinking, "I'll never write like so-and-so," or "the novel in my mind was so much better than the one on the page," make a conscious decision to be your own best critic.

Return to this workbook, and read the lines you've underlined. Go ahead. Say them aloud. You wrote those words. They're yours.

About

Novel Starter: 50 Days of Exercises and Advice to Get Your Novel off the Ground, was created by Michelle Richmond for Fiction Attic Press. Michelle is the New York Times bestselling author of five novels: *The Year of Fog, Golden State, No One You Know,* and *Dream of the Blue Room,* and the award-winning story collections *The Girl in the Fall-Away Dress* and *Hum.* She is the founder of Fiction Attic Press.

Michelle has taught in the MFA programs in creative writing at the University of San Francisco and California College of the Arts and has served as Distinguished Visiting Writer at St. Mary's College of Moraga, Bowling Green State University, and Notre Dame de Namur University. She has also taught creative writing online for Stanford Continuing Studies.

Visit her on the web at michellerichmond.com.

Find out about classes and services for writers at bookdoctor.org.

More Resources for Writing Your Novel

- The Paperclip Method: Structuring Your Novel Without an Outline
- Novel Planning Worksheets: https://gum.co/yqGuh

Made in the USA
Middletown, DE
03 June 2018